CAPITALIZATION

Teaching correct capitalization
to kids who aren't crazy
about writing in the first place

Cheryl Miller Thurston

illustrated by Zach Howard

Routledge
Taylor & Francis Group

NEW YORK AND LONDON

First published in 2000 by Prufrock Press Inc.

Published 2021 by Routledge
605 Third Avenue, New York, NY 10017
2 Park Square, Milton Park, Abingdon, Oxon OX14 4RN

Routledge is an imprint of the Taylor & Francis Group, an informa business

ISBN 13: 978-1-877673-43-6 (pbk)

Table of contents

A note to teachers

Dear Teachers:

Capitalization is not the most exciting topic in the world to teach. Oh, there are more boring subjects for English teachers (adverbial clauses and participial phrases come to mind), but capitalization is not likely to leap to the top of any teacher's list of "My Favorite Units to Teach."

It doesn't have to be that way. It is perfectly possible to teach students to capitalize correctly, without having them fall asleep over their text—if you are using a text designed with real kids in mind, and if there is some room for them to exercise their own creativity. I believe that students can have some fun with writing and, at the same time, learn to follow the rules of writing.

You will find that the activities in this book are short and always involve student writing, as well as practice sentences for students to correct. Use the activities all at once in a capitalization unit, or spread them out over several weeks. Use the review exercises throughout the year to reinforce what students have learned.

I hope the activities will work for you. They are a little strange, perhaps, but then I've found that most middle school students are a little strange, too—in a good way! Your students will have some fun with the activities as they learn to recognize and apply the rules of capitalization, one step at a time.

Sincerely,
Cheryl Miller Thurston

Who needs punctuation, capitalization and spelling, anyway?

Students often ask, "How come we have to do this stuff?" Here's one exercise that will help answer that question, at least as it relates to learning the rules of writing.

Announce to students that they are to complete the instructions below, *exactly*. (You may photocopy the instructions or put them on an overhead projector.) See how many students can complete the instructions in a set period of time, probably 15-30 minutes, depending upon the age and skill level of the students. Allow students to work in small groups, if you wish, to help each other decipher the instructions.

Be sure to have crayons, colored pencils or markers available in the room. The instructions include writing certain words in different colors.

If, at the end of the allotted time, students are still actively engaged in figuring out the instructions, consider letting them continue until at least some of the students have completed the exercise.

Who needs punctuation, capitalization and spelling, anyway?

Complete the instructions below, .

taykea pEasa nowtbuk paypur Und fould it in haFF sew that yew havva lown thinn peacea PaepPre whithh a folld ontha left cinda LIECKA greden kardd ownlee thinre riete thu wurddz OLLA bowt me awn thu fRunte inn leddres eggsacktlee won innche hi kuller the leturz gren half ewe evur cen the coLre Oven armee eweniforM thatt izthe ckuler Ewe shUd ewse wen u r dun kullureng the leDurs on thu frontt opunn the paypper lik abuk so that thu fowlde is in the middddddddul ovthe paj nou rit yer furste und LASSSSTTTT nam inNSeid in to inche hi leddres kullir thez ledERZ WreD then uzZin a bloo kraEYoN or kolURd pennsUl or mArcURR wreyte inthe daeT uf yer burth iffyu wantt draw ina piCKcher Unndur the dayte now yu R finished.

Who needs punctuation, capitalization and spelling, anyway?

Part II

The directions you just followed (or tried to follow!) were written without proper capitalization, spelling or punctuation. Most people have a very hard time figuring it out. Here is how the paragraph *should* look:

> *Take a piece of notebook paper and fold it in half so that you have a long thin piece of paper with a fold on the left, kind of like a greeting card, only thinner. Write the words "All About Me" on the front in letters exactly one inch high. Color the letters green. (Have you ever seen the color of an army uniform? That is the color you should use when you are coloring the letters on the front.)*
>
> *Open the paper like a book so that the fold is in the middle of the paper. Now write your first and last name inside in two-inch high letters. Color these letters red. Then, using a blue crayon or colored pencil or marker, write in the date of your birth. If you want, draw in a picture under the date.*
>
> *Now you are finished.*

How did you do at following the instructions? Even if you were able to complete them, it would have been much easier for you—and quicker—if you had received the set of instructions above. You would have spent your time following the directions, instead of trying to figure out what the directions said.

We have spelling, punctuation and capitalization rules because, believe it or not, they make our lives easier. When we speak, a pause or a look or a tone of voice can help convey the meaning we want. When we write, we don't have any of that to help us. The words alone must convey the meaning.

Agreeing on certain rules helps make things clearer. If the word *paper* is spelled *payper, pappur, paepre, peypar, paypur* or *paipyr,* we have to go to a lot more work when we read. We don't immediately recognize the word because it looks different each time we see it. If we agree to spell it one way, the word is easier to recognize.

In the same way, punctuation helps us sort out a traffic jam of words. The periods, question marks, commas, etc., provide road markers for us. They help divide the mass of words into something we can grab hold of. Capital letters also help. They are like road signs, highlighting a name or pointing out the beginning of a new sentence.

Think for a minute of all the customs, laws and regulations we have today to manage the automobile. Imagine what our world would be like without them. People would be able to drive and park wherever they wanted, on sidewalks, across front lawns, through playgrounds. They could drive on the left or the right side of the road, as fast or as slow as they wanted. No one would signal. There would be no traffic lights, stop signs or yield signs. No signs would identify streets, highways or exits. It would be chaos!

Just as rules help keep traffic somewhat in control, capitalization, punctuation and spelling rules help keep written language in control. Without them, every paragraph we read would be a new challenge!

The easiest rule in the world

One of the easiest rules in the world to follow is one that doesn't make much sense when you think about it. Here it is:

Capitalize the word "I."

The word *me* isn't capitalized. The word *you* isn't capitalized. The one-letter word *a* isn't capitalized. Only the word *I* is capitalized. Why?

That's a good question. According to some, it has something to do with the way typographers originally had to typeset books in the early days of printing. However, the truth is that the real reason isn't important anymore. The important thing is just to know that the word is *always* capitalized.

Example

"Yes, I am an eyeball, and I like being an eyeball," said Eyezac.

Start out easy with capitalizing practice by putting capitals where they belong in the following sentences:

1. "Well," said Simon, "if i had to pick a favorite movie song, i think it would be *The Man with the Golden Eye*, from an old James Bond movie.

2. Noah said, "i looked her in the eye, and i said, 'i don't care if i ever see you again as long as i live!'"

3. Hannah was mad. "How dare you serve me a fish head with the eyes still in it! Eyes are not something i want looking at me when i eat!"

Write:

Now write three sentences of your own. Use the word "I" at least three times and the word "eye" at least three times, total.

The second easiest rule in the world— with complications

A very easy rule for most people to remember is this one:

Capitalize the first word of a sentence.

It seems so easy. You may even be tempted to think, "Oh, please! Everyone knows that."

Most of the time it *is* easy, as in the following paragraph:

Caleb's older brother is always writing mushy love letters to his girlfriend, Marissa. Unfortunately, he also leaves them lying around while he is composing them. The letters are so mushy, they make Caleb sick.

Sometimes the rule is not quite as easy as it seems. If the sentence you are writing includes a quotation that is itself another sentence, you have a sentence within a sentence. That may sound a little confusing, but it's not. First, take a look at a plain old sentence:

In one letter, Caleb's brother told Marissa that she was beautiful.

Now suppose that we change that sentence so that it includes the exact words that Caleb's brother used—in other words, a quotation:

In one letter, Caleb's brother wrote, "My darling, you are as beautiful as butterfly wings fluttering through a dewy meadow."

Now we have a sentence that contains another sentence—the sentence that Caleb's brother actually used. The first word of *both* sentences is capitalized. "In" is capitalized because it is the first word of the whole sentence. "My" is capitalized because it is the first word of the sentence that Caleb's brother wrote.

Add capital letters, as needed, to the following:

1. when Caleb looked at his brother's letter, he said, "this stuff about butterfly wings is so disgusting."

2. his brother just got a dreamy look on his face. He said, "someday when you have found true love, you will understand."

3. caleb laughed and said, "if you think i'm ever going to tell a girl she looks like butterfly wings, you're nuts."

Write:
What else might make Caleb sick about his brother's letters? Write at least three sentences, explaining. Be sure to capitalize correctly.

Being proper about proper nouns

Sometimes rules sound so simple. For example, "Capitalize proper nouns," sounds pretty simple.

And it is—if you know what a proper noun is. But what if you don't even know what a noun is, let alone a proper noun? How can you tell a proper noun from an improper one?

First of all, there is no such thing as an improper noun. (Sometimes language is improper, but that's not the same thing as an improper noun. If someone starts swearing at a wedding ceremony, that is certainly improper, but it doesn't have anything to do with nouns.) The two kinds of nouns are *proper nouns* and *common nouns*.

Let's back up, though. Just in case you have forgotten, a noun is a person, place, thing or idea. It is a *something*.

Here are a whole bunch of nouns:

boy	fender	Fido
car	puppy	oil
wheel	Corvette	happiness
Jeffrey	danger	gasoline
Atlanta	keychain	Porsche

All of these are *things*, though two of them can't be seen. (Happiness and danger are things you can't see— but they are still nouns.)

Notice that five of the nouns are capitalized. They are the *proper* nouns. A proper noun is the name of a certain, specific noun, rather than the name of a whole class of things. The word "boy" is a noun that describes males. It is a common noun. "Jeffrey" is the name of a certain, specific boy. It is a proper noun. "Jeffrey" needs to be capitalized, but "boy" does not.

Similarly, "puppy" is a common noun, but "Fido" is a proper noun. The word "city" is a common noun, but "Atlanta" is a proper noun.

Capitalize all the proper nouns below.

shirt	television	ford	speedometer
lebron james	miley cyrus	porsche	hubcap
spaghetti	burger king	engine	exxon
argentina	volkswagen	road	drag strip
llama	van	pennsylvania turnpike	traffic ticket
basketball	sport utility vehicle	axle	frog
book	pick-up truck		

Write:

1. Take any five of the nouns above and use them in *one* sentence of your own. Be sure to capitalize correctly.

2. Write a sentence of your own that involves a car in some way—and that has at least three proper nouns. Remember to capitalize correctly.

3. Suppose you could design a car of the future. What would you design? Draw your car and write a short description of it. In your description, be sure to include the name of the car and, even though you are probably sick of being reminded about this, be sure to capitalize correctly!

Capitalize a Mexican chef
(and all proper adjectives)

A proper adjective is simply an adjective made from a proper noun. Like a proper noun, it should be capitalized.

It's possible that you are sighing and thinking, "Oh, great. I don't remember what an ordinary adjective is, let alone a proper adjective." If so, don't worry. It's very easy, really.

An adjective is a describing word. Here are a bunch of adjectives that could describe the noun *chef*:

talented chef, *hard-working* chef, *crabby* chef, *temperamental* chef

All the adjectives above are ordinary adjectives.

Now suppose that the chef is a *Mexican* chef who reads *Shakespearean* sonnets in his spare time. *Mexican* is a proper adjective. That's because it is made from the proper noun "Mexico." *Shakespearean* is also a proper adjective that describes sonnets. It is made, of course, from the proper noun "Shakespeare."

If you know that you should capitalize proper nouns, it's easy to remember to capitalize proper adjectives.

Add capital letters, as needed, to the following:

1. the new mexican chef at the chinese restaurant upset the owners when he told them the special for the day was an austrian dish with italian spaghetti sauce.

2. "you can't make european dishes in a chinese restaurant!" the owner cried. "it's downright un-american!"

3. "i'll cook what i want to cook!" said the stubborn chef. "i will go to work in the greek restaurant down the block if you don't appreciate my services."

4. "maybe, instead, you should go work at the fast food restaurant on the corner. I think you would be happier flipping burgers," said the owner, making a herculean effort to control his temper.

5. "wait," interrupted a customer, overhearing. "does this mean i can't have french dressing on my salad?"

6. "we don't even *have* salad!" sighed the owner.

Write:

What happened next? What did the chef do? What did the owner do? What did the customer do? Write three more sentences involving the chef. Be sure to use at least four proper adjectives.

Capitalize Mount Everest
(and other specific geographical names)

You probably know what geography is—the study of places and natural features, like *countries, states, mountain ranges, lakes,* etc.

Notice that all the words in the list just mentioned are nouns. Notice also that they are not capitalized. That's because we are talking about countries, states, mountain ranges, lakes, etc., in general. When we write about a *specific* country, state, mountain range, river or lake, the name should be capitalized.

Examples:

common nouns	proper nouns
country	Canada
mountain range	Rocky Mountains
lake	Lake Ontario
state	Florida
river	Mississippi River

Hint: Words like "river" and "mountain" used as part of a name *are* capitalized. For example, in Rocky Mountains, "Mountains" is considered part of the name. More examples: Ohio River, Boyd Lake, Grand Canyon.

Add capital letters, as needed, to the following:

1. kevin has climbed many hills, but he is not planning to hike up pikes peak in colorado.

2. kevin's girlfriend Sara has already climbed mount everest, as well as mount mckinley in alaska and mount kilimanjaro in tanzania.

3. she has also kayaked on many rivers, including the colorado river in arizona and the snake river in idaho.

4. she has also gone deep sea diving off the coast of mexico and sky diving in new york and toronto.

5. she has also biked in moab, utah, and across the sahara desert in africa and around mount rainier in washington.

6. sometimes kevin is very jealous of his girlfriend.

Write:

Write three more sentences about Kevin and Sara. Be sure to mention at least four specific geographical names.

Capitalize Saturday
(and days of the week, months of the year and holidays)

Imagine that you wake up in the morning on a regular day in any old month. Nothing special is happening.

The words "morning" and "day" and "month" are common nouns. They don't refer to anything special or specific.

But suppose you wake up on Thursday morning in the month of November and it is also Thanksgiving Day. Then you've got a *bunch* of capitalization that ought to go on. Thursday is a particular day with a particular name. It should be capitalized. November is a particular month with a particular name. It should be capitalized. Thanksgiving is a particular holiday with a particular name. It should be capitalized.

The rule is this: *Capitalize the names of days of the week, months of the year and holidays.*

> **Tip**
> Your birthday may be special to you, but it is capitalized. That's because it doesn't have a special name. The same term, , applies to everyone.

Add capital letters, as needed, to the following:

1. claire loves saturdays and sundays because she doesn't have to go to school.

2. claire's favorite months are june, july and august. those are the months she doesn't have to go to school.

3. claire doesn't like school very much. she also doesn't like her little brother spencer, valentine's day, scary movies, the color pink or split pea soup.

4. actually, claire doesn't like much of anything except sitting around and watching television.

5. claire is a couch potato. If she had more energy, she would support the movement to designate february 28 as national couch potato day.

Write:
Now write three sentences about Claire's brother spencer, who is not at all like Claire. Be sure to mention a month, a day of the week and a holiday.

Capitalize Portuguese Presbyterians
(and other languages and religions)

Names of languages are always capitalized. People speak French, English, Cherokee or Japanese, for example.

Names of religions and religious denominations are also capitalized. People may be Christian, Hindu, Muslim, Catholic, Baptist, Methodist, Mormon, or many other faiths.

How do you remember this? There is no easy way. One idea is to use memory hints. Here's a memory hint for remembering to capitalize religions: Think about how important religion is to so many people. Wars have even been fought over religions. Something that important needs a capital letter to indicate its importance.

See if you can come up with a memory hint for remembering to capitalize languages:

_____

_____

_____

Add capital letters, as needed, to the following:

1. emily loves cats. her favorite cat is carlos. she always speaks spanish to carlos because he was born in spain.

2. she doesn't think he understands english.

3. "carlos is also catholic," she told her friend lynn, who happens to be buddhist. "i think i will take him to visit a priest some day soon. carlos told me he would like that."

4. "cats can't be catholic," said lynn. "they don't belong to churches."

5. emily was stubborn. "carlos does. he told me he converted from lutheranism."

6. "he did not!" sniffed lynn.

7. "oh, how do you know?" said emily. "you don't speak spanish!"

Write:

Write three sentences about Emily's *other* pet. Mention at least one language and one religion.

Don't capitalize directions

When you write, "Turn right at the intersection," you probably don't think of capitalizing the word "right." That's correct. You shouldn't. So why would you think of capitalizing the word "west" in this sentence: "Turn west at the intersection"?

If you wouldn't think of it, that's good. However, many people do. For some reason, they think that the names of geographical directions are capitalized. They are not.

Perhaps some of the confusion comes from the fact that the names of the directions on the compass are also sometimes used to name areas of a country. For example, if you write, "Eliza grew up in the South on a plantation," you *do* capitalize the word "South." However, that's not because it's the name of a direction. It's because it's the name of a place—an area of the United States. The confusion comes from the direction and the area having the same name.

Here is another example:

When the Andersons were traveling west on the interstate for their family vacation in Colorado, they talked excitedly about the cowboys and horses they were going to see. When they arrived in the West, they were disappointed to see mostly busy moms driving their kids to soccer practice in sport utility vehicles.

Add capital letters, as needed, to the following:

1. The andersons were from the east. they didn't know much about life in the west, except for what they had seen in old movies on television.

2. after their disappointment at seeing no stagecoaches, sheriffs or posses in colorado, they decided to travel north to montana. they wanted to see bears.

3. they settled into a motel in the north part of billings. then they peeked out the window, looking for the bears.

4. the only animal they saw was a poodle. the lady in the unit next to theirs was trying to sneak it into her room.

5. the andersons found that the west wasn't nearly as exciting as they had thought. they decided to get on the road early and travel east back toward the land they knew best—new jersey.

Write:

Write three more sentences about the Andersons' trip. Include any of the words *north*, *south*, *east* or *west* at least three times.

Don't capitalize math
(and most other school subjects)

People get confused about what school subjects to capitalize. The thing to remember is this: Generally, you *don't* capitalize school subjects.

Okay, there are some exceptions. You *do* capitalize *English* and *Spanish* and *French*. But that's not because they are school subjects. It's because they are formed from the names of languages, which are always capitalized. "English" is capitalized because it is also the name of a language.

You capitalize English when you write, "I'm going to my English class now." But you *don't* capitalize *math* when you write, "I'm going to go to my *math* class now."

There is another kind of exception. If you are taking the name of a class that has a special title, you capitalize the name of that class. You might sign up for "Computers in the 21st Century." That is a class with a special title, similar to a book title. Here are some other examples:

    not capitalized: algebra
    capitalized: Advanced Calculus III
    not capitalized: physical education
    capitalized: Advanced Weightlifting for Non-Majors

Add capital letters, as needed, to the following:

1. nicholas failed algebra. he failed biology. he even failed art.

2. he passed his english and german classes, though. he got a "D" in both.

3. his parents said, "nicholas is gifted. that is the problem. he is just bored."

4. his teachers laughed. "nicholas is lazy," they said. "he is intelligent, but he does absolutely no work of any kind at school, ever."

5. his parents said, "no. he is brilliant. we are going to sign him up for more challenging classes. next semester he will take introduction to theories of linguistics, anatomy, russian, and developing third world nations in the new millenium.

6. nicholas failed everything.

7. the next semester, he signed himself up for introduction to underwater basket weaving.

8. he passed.

Write:
Write three more sentences about Nicholas or his family. Include at least four school subjects.

Capitalize the Civil War
(and other historical events)

What does the Civil War have to do with English? Nothing—except that it can help you remember to capitalize specific historical names. Historical names are all those special events that appear in history books, like the Civil War, the Middle Ages, the Revolutionary War, the Renaissance, the Persian Gulf War and the War of the Roses.

Now don't think that names of *general* historical events get capitalized. We don't capitalize "war." There have been thousands of wars throughout history. We *do* capitalize the name of a certain one, like the Civil War.

We *don't* capitalize the word "treaty" or "battle." We *do* capitalize Paris Peace Treaty and Battle of Verdun.

Add capital letters, as needed, to the following:

1. andrew and ashley stepped into a time travel machine and traveled back to world war I.

2. they managed to wind up right in the middle of the battle of the somme and barely managed to escape.

3. they decided they didn't like being around wars, so they went further back in time and wound up at the boston tea party.

4. "this is violent, too," said ashley. "Let's go back to the renaissance and look at famous paintings and sculptures."

5. "I don't know," said andrew. "who wants to see a bunch of paintings? instead, let's try going forward." reluctantly, ashley agreed.

6. Soon they found themselves dodging laser beamatroid bombs being dropped from a spectrorocket skimming along at the speed of light. "Where are we?" cried ashley to a humatron crouching with her under a thermospecter shield. She wished she were somewhere back in time, maybe at the battle of bull run.

7. "gazooklesnitz!" sniffed the humatron, looking down his nose at her. "haven't you ever heard of the millenium interplanetary war of the worlds? This is the war's final battle, the battle of arzepicon."

Write:

Write three more sentences about traveling in the time machine. Be sure to include at least four historical events or time periods.

Seasons are not months

Most of us know that you are supposed to capitalize months of the year. January is capitalized. June is capitalized. September is capitalized, etc.

Unfortunately, many people then think that the seasons (spring, summer, winter, fall) are also capitalized.

They are not.

Why not?

Who knows? It's just one of those things. It might help you to think that a season isn't special or unique enough to be capitalized. The season *spring*, for example, has several months in it. The months get capitalized. The season does not.

Another way to remember the rule is to note that months are often named after people or gods—and names, of course, are always capitalized. August, for example, was named after the Roman ruler Emperor Augustus. January was named after the Roman god, Janus.

Seasons weren't named after anyone. They don't get capitalized.

Add capital letters, as needed, to the following:

1. every fall, jack celebrates his pet frog's birthday on october 15. starting in september, he collects flies in a little jar as a special treat for alfred.

2. he celebrates his pet slug's birthday in the summer, on june 30. this celebration is pretty quiet, though. there's not much you can do to entertain a slug.

3. the most lively celebration occurs every winter when he celebrates his pet tarantula's birthday on february 10. as a special treat, he lets Margaret out of her cage for a few minutes in the school cafeteria.

4. every year, beginning on february 11, jack has detention for a week.

Write:
Write three more sentences about pet birthdays. Use the names of at least two seasons and two months.

Brand names are special

Brand names are the names that companies assign to the products they sell (and usually advertise—a lot). When a company puts a lot of time and money into making and selling a product, it wants that product to be special. A capital letter is just one way to indicate that it is supposed to be unique.

Take a look at just one product: corn flakes. Lots of companies make corn flakes. Therefore, the words "corn flakes" are not capitalized when you write about them. However, the brand name of the corn flakes is capitalized. Here's an example:

> Tony wanted corn flakes for breakfast. He grabbed a box of *Post Toasties* corn flakes and poured himself a bowl. His sister Kate wanted some juice. She looked in the refrigerator and was glad to see some *Tropicana*.

An interesting fact about brand names: Companies want a product to become very popular. However, there is a problem if it becomes *too* popular and people start using its name as the generic name for the product. Eventually, the company could lose its trademark protection. For example, the former trademark "Aspirin" used to be owned by the Bayer company. The product became so popular that the name "aspirin" became the generic name of the pain-reliever. Now any company can manufacture aspirin—which is no longer capitalized.

Companies try to guard against their trademarks becoming generic names. That's why the Xerox Company encourages people to use the word "photocopy" instead of "Xerox" when they refer to making reproductions. They don't want "Xerox" to become a synonym for "photocopy."

Add capital letters, as needed, to the following:

1. kate and tony's little sister hannah likes to eat gerber baby food for breakfast, usually with milk, some apple juice and a few cheerios.

2. actually, she doesn't like to eat so much as fling the food around the room. strained peaches are always landing on things—the floor, the sugar bowl, kate's new tommy hilfiger shirt, and tony's homework.

3. sometimes kate and tony just can't take it anymore. Their father takes pity on them and says, "Let's leave hannah with Mom and go get an egg mcmuffin."

4. hannah usually tosses a handful of cheerios at them on their way out to the jeep cherokee.

Write:

What happens on the way to get an Egg McMuffin? Write three sentences, and mention at least ten brand names.

When do you capitalize your relatives?

Sometimes you capitalize your relatives, and sometimes you don't—and it has nothing to do with the relatives. It does have to do with how you are using the relative's "title."

If you are using the word "dad" or "aunt" or "mother" instead of the person's name, then you capitalize the word.

Here's an example:

When Dad heard the doorbell ring, he saw that it was Aunt Mathilda on the front steps. Quickly, Mother ran to hide in the closet.

If words like *my, your, his* or *our* are used with the relative's title, then you are not using the title as a name. Then the word is *not* capitalized.

Here's an example:

When *my* dad heard the doorbell ring, he saw that it was *my* aunt on the front steps. Quickly, *my* mother ran to hide in the closet.

Add capital letters, as needed, to the following:

1. i have an aunt who is rather unusual. she is mom's sister.

2. my mom says aunt mathilda is a little eccentric. my dad says she is nutty as a fruit-cake. when he says that, mom gets mad at him.

3. when aunt mathilda comes over, things always get interesting. one time she arrived wearing a football helmet and an evening gown. she was carrying a parrot in a cage and a suitcase full of homemade cookies for me.

Write:
Write three more sentences involving Aunt Mathilda. Be sure to capitalize correctly.

Capitalize World Wrestling Entertainment
(and the names of other organizations, firms, schools, churches or institutions)

Maybe you are very interested in World Wrestling Entertainment, and maybe you couldn't care less. It doesn't matter, at least when it comes to capitalization. You should capitalize *World Wrestling Entertainment* because it is the official name of an organization. You should capitalize the official titles of *any* organization.

You should also capitalize the name of any firm or business, as well as the name of any institution, like schools, churches and government bodies.

> ### Tip
>
> Tiny words like *a, an, the, for,* and *of* are not generally capitalized in a name. Here's an example:
>
> *Clyde Smellman was a member of a wrestling union called the Society for the Protection of Wrestling Rights.*

Add capital letters, as needed, to the following:

1. clarence fendlehessy wanted to form a wrestling club of people who couldn't stand smellman the smasher—sort of a reverse fan club. that's why he founded the south quebec united association of smellman the smasher haters—also known as S.Q.U.A.S.H.

2. clarence elected himself president, and then started looking for sponsors. he tried to get donations from the american medical association, the association of school principals, state farm insurance and cola international. none of them donated anything.

3. he tried to get endorsements from the president of the motion picture association and the television broadcasting association. they weren't interested.

4. clarence was frustrated. he decided to stop at sylvester herron middle school and see if he could recruit some of the kids there. the principal wouldn't even let him in the door.

5. clarence was frustrated. he decided to go to mercy community hospital after a wrestling match. there he found two wrestlers who had been squashed by smellman the smasher.

6. they signed up immediately.

Write:

Write three more sentences about wrestling. Use at least two names of organizations, firms, schools, churches or institutions.

Capitalize "The Return of the Glowing Fish Army"
(and other titles)

Titles are important. They distinguish one work of art from another. Without a title, how would horror movie fans know to go to the movie "The Return of the Glowing Fish Army" instead of "Love on Long Island"?

Because they are important, titles of works of art are capitalized (even if you don't agree that the creation should be called "art"!) Titles of movies are capitalized. Titles of books are capitalized. Titles of paintings, television programs, sculptures, plays, songs, stories, magazines and books are all capitalized.

Most of the time, you *don't* capitalize the little words *a*, *an* and *the* in a title. You also don't capitalize tiny prepositions like "in," "on," "for" and "of." (Who knows why? Perhaps some fuddy-duddy English teacher in 1792 made up the rule just to aggravate students.) There is one exception, though. If one of these words is the *first* word in the title, you go ahead and capitalize it. That's because the first and last words in a title are always capitalized, no matter what they are.

Add capital letters, as needed, to the following:

1. artists blake witherspoon and serena rizzuto worked together to create the sets for the new musical, *alligators in the sewers.*

2. musician emilio smith composed the show's hit songs, "down in the dark dank dungeon" and "let us see light!"

3. a very talented costume designer turns 122 young dancers and singers into realistic looking alligators for the show. one of the most stunning numbers is a dance number featuring the alligators. it is called "crocodile rock, rock, rocking underground."

4. people seem to love the opening number for the second act. in it, the alligators sing a song called, "singing the scales in our scaley skin."

5. a new york critic reviewed the musical in an article called "a sumptuous subterranean symphony of song." she liked the show.

6. another critic wrote a review called, "snoring in the sewer." he did not like it.

Write:

Another show is playing in the theater next door to the one where *Alligators in the Sewers* is playing. Write three sentences about this show. Include at least three titles.

Capitalize Doctor Snodgrass
(and other titles used with a name)

Just a warning: People are always getting confused by this next capitalization rule. It's not hard. It's not even confusing. However, people still manage to get it wrong.

Here's the rule:

Capitalize people's titles only when they are used with the person's name.
Don't capitalize the title when it is not used with a person's name.

Notice how the titles "aunt" and "doctor" are used in the following:

Julia went to the doctor because of her broken toe. When Doctor Snodgrass saw her toe, he said, "I think we will need to amputate."

Julia turned green, and her aunt caught her just before she fell.

"Oops," said the doctor. "I was just kidding."

"You are also fired," said Aunt Bea.

Add capital letters, as needed, to the following:

1. julia's uncle drove her and her aunt to find another doctor who didn't have a sick sense of humor. they decided on doctor martinez. "she sounds like a good doctor," said uncle pete. "our neighbor, general gutting, likes her a lot, and reverend matthew from our church does, too."

2. they went into the doctor's office and smiled. they were glad to see that doctor martinez looked very kind. her receptionist looked kind. the nurse looked kind. even the man repairing the photocopy machine looked kind.

3. julia held out her foot. "hmmmmmmm," said the doctor. "i think it's appendicitis," she said, smiling.

4. julia was not amused.

Write:

Write three more sentences about Julia and her injury. In your sentences, use at least three titles like *doctor, professor, aunt, uncle, general, president, captain*, etc.

The French dressing rule

Most of us know that we should capitalize the names of countries. (If you don't know that, now is the time to learn!) Most of us also know we should capitalize languages. Yet many of us are confused when we come upon a sentence like this:

Harold put french dressing on his salad.

Do we capitalize French *and* dressing? Or just French? You capitalize only French. French is capitalized because it is a language. The word "dressing" just happens to be there. There is no reason at all to capitalize it. The sentence, therefore, should look like this:

Harold put French dressing on his salad.

Here is another example of the French dressing rule in effect:

She sold homemade blue cheese dressing to earn enough money to buy an English sheepdog named Max.

"English" is capitalized because it comes from the name of a country. There are lots of English sheepdogs around, but "Max" is capitalized because it is the name of a certain English sheepdog. Blue cheese dressing is not capitalized, because "blue cheese" doesn't come from the name of a country. Don't get confused and think that all dressings should be capitalized!

Add capital letters, as needed, to the following:

1. in college, joe signed up for a spanish class, a class on dog training and a class on french cooking—all at the same time.

2. he wants to impress a girl named maria. since she speaks only spanish, he realized some time ago that he couldn't ask her on a date until he learned spanish, too.

3. before inviting her over for dinner, he thought it would be a good idea to teach his irish springer spaniel named petunia not to jump on people, knock them over or lick their faces.

4. he thought it might also be a good idea to learn how to cook something besides boiled hot dogs and salad from a bag topped with russian dressing.

5. joe is studying very, very hard. He wants to ask maria for a date before she gets too serious about the german exchange student she has been smiling at so much lately.

Write:

Write three more sentences about Joe. Use at least two examples of the French dressing rule in your sentences.

Capitalize the Empire State Building
(and the name of any other particular person, place or thing)

Actually, this rule is a repeat. It's just another way of saying, "Capitalize proper nouns." The Empire State Building is a proper noun. So are these words: Fido, the Milky Way, Harley Davidson, and New Year's Eve. They are all the names of *particular* persons, places or things.

Remember, you don't capitalize the name of a whole class of things, like, for example, "puppies." But you *do* capitalize the name of a particular puppy, like "FuFu."

Add capital letters, as needed, to the following:

imagine the problems that would take place if dinosaurs ad not become extinct. can you imagine a herd of dinosaurs ving in new york city? people in the empire state building night gaze out their windows into the eyes of a dinosaur. an ccordion player entertaining on the corner of madison avenue and 37th street might be squashed by the foot of a dinoaur named bill who doesn't appreciate fine music. one sweep f a dinosaur tail could send a fleet of cars sailing into the udson river or the atlantic ocean or radio city music hall. television commercials would advertise a product called dynamite inosaur repellent. a best-selling book would be *trapped in the ronx*, the story of one family's battle against a dinosaur that onsidered himself to be the family's adopted pet, ralphie.

one woman, general rita m. fazio, would become famous or leading the u.s. army in the great predator battle of 2031, hich students taking history classes would study for generations to come. she would discover that dinosaurs love saxophone music and order hornsbie to play the great blues hit of 2031, "my apartment building was crushed by a dinosaur," while troops protected him with tanks and artillery. The dinosaurs would all come out to hear him. He would march out of town, and they would follow, just like the children followed the pied piper in the old fairy tale, "the pied piper of hamelin." soon all the dinosaurs would be living in connecticut.

the people of new york would rejoice.

Write:

What would happen to the people in Connecticut? Write 3 sentences, continuing the story. Use at least 10 capital letters correctly in your sentences.

After the station wagon broke down

Add capital letters, as needed, to the following:

1. pete's grandpa needed a new car. the station wagon that had 238,000 miles on it finally broke down in a walmart parking lot.

2. pete asked, "what are you going to get, grandpa? a ford? a chevrolet? a mercedes?

3. his grandfather just smiled. "i have something else in mind, something I saw advertised on the television special, 'adventures at the north pole.' what i have in mind is the latest thing."

4. "does it get good gas mileage?"pete asked.

5. "no, but it flies," said grandpa. "we can avoid all that traffic on college avenue by just buzzing right over it. plus, I think it will attract cute girls."

6. "grandpa!" said pete, shocked.

7. "i'm thinking of you, pete," said his grandfather. "don't *you* want to attract cute girls?"

8. "well, yes," said pete. "There's one in my math class, especially."

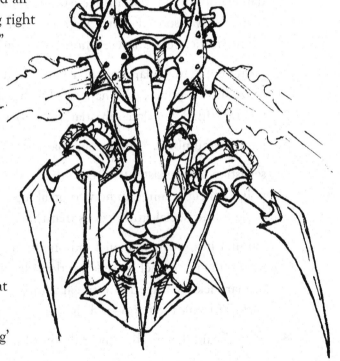

9. "wait until she sees you buzzing along with me in the transflyer acg II," said grandpa. "we can buzz over thomas mayhew middle school after school, and i'll bet anything that girl will notice you."

10. "Hmmmmm," said pete. "what does the 'acg' stand for, anway?"

11. "I think it's for 'attracts cute girls,'" said grandpa.

Write:

Next Pete went to his grandmother, who had also been looking for a new car to replace the station wagon. Write a paragraph telling about his grandmother's choice for a car. Use at least 10 capital letters correctly in your sentences.

Dancing Daniel

Add capitals, as needed, to the following:

1. daniel was walking north down the street one spring saturday afternoon, minding his own business, when he heard it— his favorite song in the world, "amanabanna moves," by his favorite group, flannel pizza dough.

2. the music was coming from the patio of the italian restaurant, claudio's, located on martinelli street in between a baptist elementary school and borg's appliance and refrigeration service.

3. daniel couldn't help it. his feet started moving, and he shouted, "this is *it*, man!" he was soon dancing, leaping, spinning, doing flips and singing along to the music. he didn't even notice that quite a crowd was gathering.

4. soon people were clapping their hands and singing along with daniel. his older sister jennifer, who happened to be eating with her date at claudio's, was mortified. her date sebastian said, "hey, isn't that your brother?"

5. jennifer mumbled, "i never saw that kid before in my life."

6. sebastian was persistent. "i really do think it's your brother," he said. "oh, look. there's a police officer coming up now to break up the crowd. it's officer hosek, the policeman who came to our social studies class that time."

7. jennifer just groaned. daniel did one final spin as the music ended, and the crowd burst into applause. daniel bowed and then decided to show off a little by doing one more spectacular kick. he leaped into the air, flung out his foot and managed to knock officer hosek backward into the patio—and right into sebastian's plate of spaghetti.

8. "oops," said daniel. the officer did not look amused. neither did jennifer. neither did sebastian.

9. daniel quickly figured out that he might be in a bit of trouble. "there's my sister!" he said. "jennifer! help me! call mom!"

10. jennifer just glared at him. she repeated her earlier words to sebastian: "i never saw this kid before in my life."

Write:

What happens next? Write one more paragraph, continuing the story above. Use at least ten capital letters correctly in your sentences.

The . . . . . . ?

What is pictured below? Where was it sighted? By whom? When? What direction was it traveling? What was it doing? What else do you know about it?

Answer these questions in a paragraph that includes at least 25 capital letters. Yes, they must be capital letters that are used correctly!

25

A test

Bug attack

Add capital letters, as needed, to the following:

1. everyone has heard of computer bugs. of course camilla had, too. she was surprised, however, to see a computer bug actually crawl out of the monitor one day and sit on her mouse.

2. she was even more surprised when the bug started talking. she stared in shock when the bug said, "you really ought to get rid of that game you are playing. you need a new game, and i have invented it. it's called bug attack, and i'm trying to get bill gates to sell it as a microsoft product."

3. camilla just stared. she had never heard of a computer bug that looked like an actual bug. she had certainly never heard a bug talk before. she didn't know what to say.

4. the bug sighed. "cat got your tongue?" he asked.

5. "no-oo-ooo," said camilla nervously. she looked around for a cat. if computer bugs could come out of the computer, then maybe cats really could grab a person's tongue.

6. "i'll make it easy for you," said the bug. "my name is harold. you need to be nice to me. i can get inside your computer and make your life miserable. in fact, i can even give you this new australian virus. it started near the great barrier reef and quickly spread to computers in sydney, then north to the united states and the rest of the world."

7. "um..." said camilla. she didn't want a computer virus, so she tried to be nice. she gave the bug a half-hearted smile. "well...maybe I could buy bug attack, but I really just like playing jupiter space race and barbie the fashion astronaut."

8. the bug groaned. "buy bug attack. it's only $583.00 and well worth the money. your birthday is coming up on saturday, november 11. you could ask for the game for a birthday present."

9. camilla frowned. "my parents would never spend $583.00 on a birthday present! even my rich uncle duke wouldn't spend that much on me."

10. "too bad," said harold, gesturing toward the monitor. more bugs crawled out and started walking all over everything. "here are some of my friends. maybe they can talk you into this."

11. "i don't have the money!" cried camilla.

12. "but you have a rich uncle duke," said the bug. "what does he do?"

13. "he is president of the united conglomeration of conglomerates. he works in the empire state building," she began.

14. "tell me more." the bugs looked eager.

15. "well...he's catholic. he likes to go to the opera. the barber of seville is his favorite opera. he also likes old reruns of 'the brady bunch.' he's married. he has three children and a frog."

16. "frogs! yuk!" cried the bugs. "we hate frogs."

17. camilla smiled a wicked grin. "well, then you probably won't like calvin, my frog. just a minute and I'll get him."

18. the bugs hightailed it back into the monitor.

Write:

And then what happened? Add at least one more paragraph to the story. Use at least ten correctly capitalized words.

ANSWER KEYS

The easiest rule, page 4

1. "Well," said Simon, "if I had to pick a favorite movie song, I think it would be "The Man with the Golden Eye," from an old James Bond movie.

2. Noah said, "I looked her in the eye, and I said, 'I don't care if I ever see you again as long as I live!'"

3. Hannah was mad. "How dare you serve me a fish head with the eyes still in it! Eyes are not something I want looking at me when I eat!"

Write:

Answers will vary. Here are some possibilities.

"Did you see that they now have contacts that can make your eyes look really weird?" asked Rhonda. "You can have dollar signs instead of pupils. You can have plaid or flowered eyes. You can even get contacts that make your eyes look bloodshot."

"That's silly," said Patty. "I can get bloodshot eyes just by trying to get all the homework done for Mr. Bauserman's class each night."

"I guess they are pretty silly. I don't know why anyone would want to look like they have been up all night doing homework," said Rhonda.

The second easiest rule, page 5

When Caleb looked at his brother's letter, he said, "This stuff about butterfly wings is so disgusting."

His brother just got a dreamy look on his face. He said, "Someday when you have found true love, you will understand."

Caleb laughed and said, "If you think I'm ever going to tell a girl she looks like butterfly wings, you're nuts."

Write:

Answers will vary. Here are some possibilities.

Caleb's brother wrote, "Marissa, you are the sunshine in all of my days and the moonlight in all my nights." Caleb gagged. "My love for you is bigger than any solar system," the letter continued, "and more infinite than the universe."

Caleb stopped reading. He couldn't take any more.

Being proper about proper nouns, page 6

shirt, LeBron James, spaghetti, Argentina, llama, basketball, book, television, Miley Cyrus, Burger King, Volkswagen, van, sport utility vehicle, pick-up truck, Ford, Porsche, engine, road, Pennsylvania Turnpike, axle, speedometer, hubcap, Exxon, drag strip, traffic ticket, frog

Write:

Answers will vary. Here are some possibilities.

1. There was a llama eating spaghetti and watching television in the back of the pick-up truck driving on the Pennsylvania Turnpike.

2. A Porsche is a car I'd like to own when I become a famous movie star like Vanessa Hudgens or Zac Efron.

3. My car of the future would be called the OttoDrive. It would drive automatically, using a computer. It would eliminate all accidents because the computers in all cars would communicate and keep people from crashing into one another because of silly mistakes. People could just lie down and watch the TV in the ceiling of the OttoDrive.

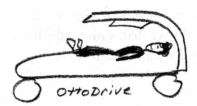
OttoDrive

Capitalize a Mexican chef, page 8

1. The new Mexican chef at the Chinese restaurant upset the owners when he told them the special for the day was an Austrian dish with Italian spaghetti sauce.

2. "You can't make European dishes in a Chinese restaurant!" the owner cried. "It's downright un-American!"

3. "I'll cook what I want to cook!" said the stubborn chef. "I will go to work in the Greek restaurant down the block if you don't appreciate my services."

4. "Maybe, instead, you should go work at the fast food restaurant on the corner. I think you would be happier flipping burgers," said the owner, making a Herculean effort to control his temper.

5. "Wait," interrupted a customer, overhearing. "Does this mean I can't have French dressing on my salad?"

6. "We don't even *have* salad!" sighed the owner.

Write:

Answers will vary. Here are some possibilities.

Realizing he didn't want to lose another customer, the owner calmed down and tried to smooth things over with the customer. "We don't have salad," he said, "but we do have delicious Chinese potstickers that we serve on a bed of iceberg lettuce."

"You can always put some sweet and sour sauce on the lettuce and that will taste a lot like Russian dressing," the chef added, "or I can mix it with a little milk to look like French dressing."

The customer was relieved. "Great," he said. "I'll have that, with a side dish of Indian curry and some Turkish coffee."

Capitalize Mount Everest, page 9

1. Kevin has climbed many hills, but he is not planning to hike up Pikes Peak in Colorado.

2. Kevin's girlfriend Sara has already climbed Mount Everest, as well as Mount McKinley in Alaska and Mount Kilimanjaro in Tanzania.

3. She has also kayaked on many rivers, including the Colorado River in Arizona and the Snake River in Idaho.

4. She has also gone deep sea diving off the coast of Mexico and sky diving in New York and Toronto.

5. She has also biked in Moab, Utah, and across the Sahara Desert in Africa and around Mount Rainier in Washington.

6. Sometimes Kevin is very jealous of his girlfriend.

Write:

Answers will vary. Here are some possibilities.

. Sara is also much better at fishing than Kevin. She has been bone-fishing in the Bahamas and fly-fishing on the North Platte River in Wyoming. She once caught a six-foot sturgeon on a fishing boat where the Pacific Ocean meets the Columbia River.

Capitalize Saturday, page 10

1. Claire loves Saturdays and Sundays because she doesn't have to go to school.

2. Claire's favorite months are June, July and August. Those are the months she doesn't have to go to school.

3. Claire doesn't like school very much. She also doesn't like her little brother Spencer, Valentine's Day, scary movies, the color pink or split pea soup.

4. Actually, Claire doesn't like much of

anything except sitting around and watching television.

5. Claire is a couch potato. If she had more energy, she would support the movement to designate February 28 as National Couch Potato Day.

Write:

Answers will vary. Here are some possibilities.

Spencer also likes Saturdays, but he thinks watching television is stupid.

Spencer's favorite month is January because then he can spend his weekends skiing, sledding or snowmobiling.

This year Spencer's favorite holiday was Valentine's Day because he is so ga-ga over Clarissa, his girlfriend who also hates watching TV.

Capitalize Portuguese Presbyterians, page 11

Memory hint: Names of languages start with large letters. (Note all the "ls" here.)

1. Emily loves cats. Her favorite cat is Carlos. She always speaks Spanish to Carlos because he was born in Spain.

2. She doesn't think he understands English.

3. "Carlos is also Catholic," she told her friend Lynn, who happens to be Buddhist. "I think I will take him to visit a priest some day soon. Carlos told me he would like that."

4. "Cats can't be Catholic," said Lynn. "They don't belong to churches."

5. Emily was stubborn. "Carlos does. He told me he converted from Lutheranism."

6. "He did not!" sniffed Lynn.

7. "Oh, how do you know?" said Emily. "You don't speak Spanish!"

Write:

Answers will vary. Here are some possibilities.

"I do have a hard time communicating with my pet tarantula Boris," Emily told her friend Lynn. "He is from Romania, and I don't speak Romanian.

"Boris is also Jewish," Emily continued, "so I thought maybe he knew Hebrew or Yiddish. The problem is, I can't speak those languages either. All I know is English."

Lynn threw up her hands and said, "Emily, you may know how to speak English, but all I hear right now is nonsense."

Don't capitalize directions, page 12

1. The Andersons were from the East. They didn't know much about life in the West, except for what they had seen in old movies on television.

2. After their disappointment at seeing no stagecoaches, sheriffs or posses in Colorado, they decided to travel north to Montana. They wanted to see bears.

3. They settled into a motel in the north part of Billings. Then they peeked out the window, looking for the bears.

4. The only animal they saw was a poodle. The lady in the unit next to theirs was trying to sneak it into her room.

5. The Andersons found that the West wasn't nearly as exciting as they had thought. They decided to get on the road early and travel east back toward the land they knew best—New Jersey.

Write:

Answers will vary. Here are some possibilities.

While driving east toward New Jersey, the Andersons decided to take a little detour through Kansas to see the historic Boot Hill in Dodge City, Kansas. By travelling south from Montana to Kansas, they hoped to see at least a pretend gunfight in the streets of the historic town. However, when they got to Boot Hill, they discovered that the two gunfighters had gone on a two-week vacation back east to Pennsylvania Dutch country.

Don't capitalize math, page 13

1. Nicholas failed algebra. He failed biology. He even failed art.

2. He passed his English and German classes, though. He got a "D" in both.

3. His parents said, "Nicholas is gifted. That is the problem. He is just bored."

4. His teachers laughed. "Nicholas is lazy," they said. "He is intelligent, but he does absolutely no work of any kind at school, ever."

5. His parents said, "No. He is brilliant. We are going to sign him up for more challenging classes. Next semester he will take Introduction to Theories of Linguistics, anatomy, Russian, and Developing Third World Nations in the New Millenium.

6. Nicholas failed everything.

7. The next semester, he signed himself up for Introduction to Underwater Basket Weaving.

8. He passed.

Write:

Answers will vary. Here are some possibilities.

After that, Nicholas's parents said that he could choose his own courses. The next semester he took the Science of Watching Television, Mastering Movies and the Culinary Art of Carnival Food. He, of course, passed each one.

Nicholas bragged to his friends, "I'm on the dean's list, and I never had to crack open an algebra book."

Capitalize the Civil War, page 14

1. Andrew and Ashley stepped into a time travel machine and traveled back to World War I.

2. They managed to wind up right in the middle of the Battle of the Somme and barely managed to escape.

3. They decided they didn't like being around wars, so they went further back in time and wound up at the Boston Tea Party.

4. "This is violent, too," said Ashley. "Let's go back to the Renaissance and look at famous paintings and sculptures."

5. "I don't know," said Andrew. "Who wants to see a bunch of paintings? Instead, let's try going forward." Reluctantly, Ashley agreed.

6. Soon they found themselves dodging laser beamatroid bombs being dropped from a spectrorocket skimming along at the speed of light. "Where are we?" cried Ashley to a humatron crouching with her under a thermospecter shield. She wished she were somewhere back in time, maybe at the Battle of Bull Run.

7. "Gazooklesnitz!" sniffed the humatron, looking down his nose at her. "Haven't you ever heard of the Millenium Interplanetary War of the Worlds? This is the war's final battle, the Battle of Arzepicon.

Write:

Answers will vary. Here are some possibilities.

"Hey, Ashley," said Andrew. "I know what would be more interesting than checking out boring history stuff, like the Civil War or the Coronation of Charlemagne. Let's go back to the 1960s and see what our parents were like."

"That's a great idea, Andrew!" Ashley said. "Maybe they were cool hippies who hung out with Bob Dylan and John Lennon and protested the Vietnam War."

When they got there, Andrew was dismayed. "My parents were big nerds when they were young, too. I thought everyone was cool at least once in their lives. I wonder if I was adopted."

Seasons are not months, page 15

1. Every fall, Jack celebrates his pet frog's birthday on October 15. Starting in September, he collects flies in a little jar as a special treat for Alfred.

2. He celebrates his pet slug's birthday in the summer, on June 30. This celebration is pretty quiet, though. There's not much you can do to entertain a slug.

3. The most lively celebration occurs every winter when he celebrates his pet tarantula's birthday on February 10. As a special treat, he lets Margaret out of her cage for a few minutes in the school cafeteria.

4. Every year, beginning on February 11, Jack has detention for a week.

Write:
Answers will vary. Here are some possibilities.

I'll never forget when my cat Sweet Pea was born because it happened the same day as my birthday in April. Every spring since then, Sweet Pea and I have a birthday party together. We invite lots of kids and kittens. This summer Sweet Pea is going to have her own batch of kittens, probably sometime in June.

Brand names are special, page 16

1. Kate and Tony's little sister Hannah likes to eat Gerber baby food for breakfast, usually with milk, some apple juice and a few Cheerios.

2. Actually, she doesn't like to eat so much as fling the food around the room. Strained peaches are always landing on things—the floor, the sugar bowl, Kate's new Tommy Hilfiger shirt, and Tony's homework.

3. Sometimes Kate and Tony just can't take it anymore. Their father takes pity on them and says, "Let's leave Hannah with Mom and go get an Egg McMuffin."

4. Hannah usually tosses a handful of Cheerios at them on their way out to the Jeep Cherokee.

Write:
Answers will vary. Here are some possibilities.

The Jeep Cherokee was in the shop, so Kate, Tony and their dad had to take the Ford Pinto out to McDonald's. Kate and her dad waited in the car while Tony was inside putting on his Calvin Klein jeans, washing his face with a Bioré strip, gargling some Listerine and putting on some cool sunglasses from Target.

When they got to the restaurant, Tony smiled and swaggered to the counter where Candace was standing in her McDonald's shirt, her Doc Martens, her Gap capri pants and her Revlon Luscious Lilac lipstick.

When do you capitalize your relatives?, page 17

1. I have an aunt who is rather unusual. She is Mom's sister.

2. My mom says Aunt Mathilda is a little eccentric. My dad says she is nutty as a fruitcake. When he says that, Mom gets mad at him.

3. When Aunt Mathilda comes over, things always get interesting. One time she arrived wearing a football helmet and an evening gown. She was carrying a parrot in a cage and a suitcase full of homemade cookies for me.

Write:

Answers will vary. Here are some possibilities.

I truly love my Aunt Mathilda because she lets me try on her evening gowns and wear her fancy rhinestone jewelry. Last summer she went on a trip to Jamaica and met Hank, who is soon going to be my uncle. I get to be a bridesmaid because I'm her favorite niece, but I also have to wear a chartreuse chiffon dress with leopard skin trim.

Capitalize World Wrestling Entertainment, page 18

1. Clarence Fendlehessy wanted to form a wrestling club of people who couldn't stand Smellman the Smasher—sort of a reverse fan club. That's why he founded the South Quebec United Association of Smellman the Smasher Haters—also known as S.Q.U.A.S.H.

2. Clarence elected himself president, and then started looking for sponsors. He tried to get donations from the American Medical Association, the Association of School Principals, State Farm Insurance and Cola International. None of them donated anything.

3. He tried to get endorsements from the president of the Motion Picture Association and the Television Broadcasting Association. They weren't interested.

4. Clarence was frustrated. He decided to stop at Sylvester Herron Middle School and see if he could recruit some of the kids there. The principal wouldn't even let him in the door.

5. Clarence was frustrated. He decided to go to Mercy Community Hospital after a wrestling match. There he found two wrestlers who had been squashed by Smellman the Smasher.

6. They signed up immediately.

Write:

Answers will vary. Here are some possibilities.

My mom hates wrestling so much because it is so gross and sweaty. In fact, she hates it so much that she is starting an organization called Mothers Against Sweaty and Gross Wrestling. She held the first meeting in the basement of the Methodist church, but her friend Sally was the only other one to show up.

Capitalize "The Return of the Glowing Fish Army," page 19

1. Artists Blake Witherspoon and Serena Rizzuto worked together to create the sets for the new musical, *Alligators in the Sewers*.

2. Musician Emilio Smith composed the show's hit songs, "Down in the Dark Dank Dungeon" and "Let Us See Light!"

3. A very talented costume designer turns 122 young dancers and singers into realistic looking alligators for the show. One of the most stunning numbers is a dance number featuring the alligators. It is called "Crocodile Rock, Rock, Rocking Underground."

4. People seem to love the opening number for the second act. In it, the alligators sing a song called, "Singing the Scales in Our Scaley Skin."

5. A new york critic reviewed the musical in an article called "A Sumptuous Subterranean Symphony of Song." She liked the show.

6. Another critic wrote a review called, "Snoring in the Sewer." He did not like it.

Write:

Answers will vary. Here are some possibilities.

"Max Power's *How Green Was My Grass* was the most exciting lawn musical ever!" raved the critic from the *New York Times*. Roger Ebert said, "I didn't know a musical about grass could get any better than *The Mower Blade*, but Max Power shows that it can. This is the musical that makes grown men weep, especially when the neighborhood men sing the heart-wrenching song 'My Lawn is Brown' during the summer drought."

Capitalize Doctor Snodgrass, page 20

1. Julia's uncle drove her and her aunt to find another doctor who didn't have a sick sense of humor. They decided on Doctor Martinez. "She sounds like a good doctor," said Uncle Pete. "Our neighbor, General Gutting, likes her a lot, and Reverend Matthew from our church does, too."

2. They went into the doctor's office and smiled. They were glad to see that Doctor Martinez looked very kind. Her receptionist looked kind. The nurse looked kind. Even the man repairing the photocopy machine looked kind.

3. Julia held out her foot. "Hmmmmmmm," said the doctor. "I think it's appendicitis," she said, smiling.

4. Julia was not amused.

Write:

Answers will vary. Here are some possibilities.

Julia was heartbroken about her toe because that meant Coach Sanders would not let her play starting center halfback on the soccer team. It also meant that she would have to tell Maestro Hollandaise that she could not twirl her baton for the marching band's halftime show. Unfortunately, Julia's broken toe was not going to get her out of writing the paper on foot fungus that was due in Professor Ridenhour's class.

The French dressing rule, page 21

1. In college, Joe signed up for a Spanish class, a class on dog training and a class on French cooking—all at the same time.

2. He wants to impress a girl named Maria. Since she speaks only Spanish, he realized some time ago that he couldn't ask her on a date until he learned Spanish, too.

3. Before inviting her over for dinner, he thought it would be a good idea to teach his Irish springer spaniel named Petunia not to jump on people, knock them over or lick their faces.

4. He thought it might also be a good idea to learn how to cook something besides boiled hot dogs and salad from a bag topped with Russian dressing.

5. Joe is studying very, very hard. He wants to ask Maria for a date before she gets too serious about the German exchange student she has been smiling at so much lately.

Write:

Answers will vary. Here are some possibilities.

Joe completely forgot about Maria after he met Chloe, the teacher of his French cooking class. Chloe's English is not very good, so he quit his Spanish class and asked Chloe to teach him French while he helped her with her English.

It turns out that Chloe was really just a French cooking fraud. She only knew how to make French toast and salad with French dressing.

Capitalize the Empire State Building, page 22

Imagine the problems that would take place if dinosaurs had not become extinct. Can you imagine a herd of dinosaurs living in New York City? People in the Empire State Building might gaze out their windows into the eyes of a dinosaur. An accordion player entertaining on the corner of Madison Avenue and 37th Street might be squashed by the foot of a dinosaur named Bill who doesn't appreciate fine music. One sweep of a dinosaur tail could send a fleet of cars sailing into the Hudson River or the Atlantic Ocean or Radio City Music Hall. Television commercials would advertise a product called Dynamite Dinosaur Repellent. A best-selling book would be *Trapped in the Bronx*, the story of one family's battle against a dinosaur that considered himself to be the family's adopted pet, Ralphie.

One woman, General Rita M. Fazio, would become famous for leading the U.S. Army in the Great Predator Battle of 2031, which students taking history classes would study for generations to come. She would discover that dinosaurs love saxophone music and order Hornsbie to play the great blues hit of 2031, "My Apartment Building was Crushed by a Dinosaur," while troops protected him with tanks and artillery. The dinosaurs would all come out to hear him. He would march out of town, and they would follow, just like the children followed the Pied Piper in the old fairy tale, "The Pied Piper of Hamelin." Soon all the dinosaurs would be living in Connecticut.

The people of New York would rejoice.

Write:

Answers will vary. Here are some possibilities.

The people of Connecticut would be much more resourceful and use their good Yankee ingenuity to put the dinosaurs to work. The idea would begin with Senator McMurtry, who would decide to have the dinosaurs work for the Connecticut Department of Transportation to help build new roads for all those people commuting to New York City. The dinosaurs would help excavate with their tails and flatten road beds with their feet.

Martha Stewart, also formerly of Connecticut, would even do shows on how to use pterodactyl eggs to make German chocolate cake.

After the station wagon broke down, page 23

1. Pete's grandpa needed a new car. The station wagon that had 238,000 miles on it finally broke down in a Walmart parking lot.

2. Pete asked, "What are you going to get, Grandpa? A Ford? A Chevrolet? A Mercedes?"

3. His grandfather just smiled. "I have something else in mind, something I saw advertised on the television special, 'Adventures at the North Pole.' What I have in mind is the latest thing."

4. "Does it get good gas mileage?" Pete asked.

5. "No, but it flies," said Grandpa. "We can avoid all that traffic on College Avenue by just buzzing right over it. Plus, I think it will attract cute girls."

6. "Grandpa!" said Pete, shocked.

7. "I'm thinking of you, Pete," said his grandfather. "Don't *you* want to attract cute girls?"

8. "Well, yes," said Pete. "There's one in my math class, especially."

9. "Wait until she sees you buzzing along with me in the Transflyer ACG II," said Grandpa. "We can buzz over Thomas Mayhew Middle School after school, and I'll bet anything that girl will notice you."

10. "Hmmmmm," said Pete. "What does the 'ACG' stand for, anway?"

11. "I think it's for 'Attracts Cute Girls,'" said Grandpa.

Write:

Answers will vary. Here are some possibilities.

"Pete, honey, your grandfather is sorely mistaken, if he thinks he is getting a Transflyer ACG II," said Pete's grandma. "I'm the one who spent all those years hauling around your dad, your Aunt Marva and your Uncle Roy in that hideous station wagon. This time I'm getting what I want."

"What are you thinking of getting, Grandma?" asked Pete.

"I know exactly what I'm getting—a Lady Luck Limo. This is the perfect transportation to take me to all the casinos in Las Vegas, like the Luxor and New York, New York.

The Lady Luck Limo also comes equipped with a change machine, so I always have plenty of money for the slot machines and lavender leather seats to match my lucky outfit. Last but not least, it also comes with a complete CD collection, including Wayne Newton, Engelbert Humperdinck and Frankie Yankovic, the Polka King," Grandma explained.

"Wow, Grandma! That *does* sound pretty cool," said Pete.

Dancing Daniel, page 24

1. Daniel was walking north down the street one spring Saturday afternoon, minding his own business, when he heard it—his favorite song in the world, "Amanabanna Moves," by his favorite group, Flannel Pizza Dough.

2. The music was coming from the patio of the Italian restaurant, Claudio's, located on Martinelli Street in between a Baptist elementary school and Borg's Appliance and Refrigeration Service.

3. Daniel couldn't help it. His feet started moving, and he shouted, "This is *it*, man!" He was soon dancing, leaping, spinning, doing flips and singing along to the music. He didn't even notice that quite a crowd was gathering.

4. Soon people were clapping their hands and singing along with Daniel. His older sister Jennifer, who happened to be eating with her date at Claudio's, was mortified. Her date Sebastian said, "Hey, isn't that your brother?"

5. Jennifer mumbled, "I never saw that kid before in my life."

6. Sebastian was persistent. "I really do think it's your brother," he said. "Oh, look. There's a police officer coming up now to break up the crowd. It's Officer Hosek, the policeman who came to our social studies class that time."

7. Jennifer just groaned. Daniel did one final spin as the music ended, and the crowd burst into applause. Daniel bowed and then decided to show off a little by doing one more spectacular kick. He leaped into the air, flung out his foot and managed to knock Officer Hosek backward into the patio—and right into Sebastian's plate of spaghetti.

8. "Oops," said Daniel. The officer did not looked amused. Neither did Jennifer. Neither did Sebastian.

9. Daniel quickly figured out that he might be in a bit of trouble. "There's my sister!" he said. "Jennifer! Help me! Call Mom!"

10. Jennifer just glared at him. She repeated her earlier words to Sebastian: "I never saw this kid before in my life."

Write:

Answers will vary. Here are some possibilities.

Right then a chubby man in an Armani suit stepped up. He gave Officer Hosek his card and told him that he would make sure that Daniel didn't create any more problems. The business card simply said "Lance Chaney, Dream Maker." Officer Hosek read it and shrugged. He was about ready for his latté break, so he agreed, "Sure. Just make sure I don't have to come back here." Daniel was puzzled. He thought to himself, "My own sister won't claim me, but this perfect stranger is lending me a hand. What a good Samaritan."

"Hello, young man. Here is my card. I can make dreams come true for talent like you," said the well-dressed, well-fed man. "I'm the man behind popular music groups like Bleak House Boys and 'N Cahoots. I'm sure you've heard of them. I need talent and looks like yours for my new group Backlash. I can make you rich and famous, young man. I can make all of your dreams come true. I'm Lance Chaney, the Dream Maker."

For the first time ever, Daniel was absolutely speechless. Jennifer, however, had been listening. Suddenly, she couldn't stop telling Sebastian and all of the other diners about how close she was to her wonderful brother Daniel.

The . . . . . . ?, page 25

Answers will vary. Here is one possibility:

Fleblo is a young executive in the advertising firm Trobelia and Souse, the top firm in Minneapolis in the year 2055. He is in love with his sister Jessica's best friend Isabel. Isabel, however, doesn't even consider him a boyfriend. He has only five legs, and she prefers young men with seven legs, especially if they speak French or play basketball.

Jessica is a cook in a Siberian restaurant. Surprisingly, Siberian cooking became very popular in the year 2050. Fleblo doesn't like Siberian food, though, and neither does Isabel, so they do have something in common.

Jessica tries to get Isabel interested in Fleblo, but nothing works. Finally, Fleblo checks into Carolla Community Hospital. He's going to have a double leg attachment performed by Doctor Nicholas Proust. He hopes his new look will attract Isabel.

It doesn't. However, a nurse at the hospital falls in love with Fleblo. Luckily, he falls in love with her, too. They get married in the Unitarian Church on Garosted Avenue near the Hispwickell River. They have 23 children, all with five legs each.

Bug Attack, page 26

1. Everyone has heard of computer bugs. Of course Camilla had, too. She was surprised, however, to see a computer bug actually crawl out of the monitor one day and sit on her mouse.

2. She was even more surprised when the bug started talking. She stared in shock when the bug said, "You really ought to get rid of that game you are playing. You need a new game, and I have invented it. It's called Bug Attack, and I'm trying to get Bill Gates to sell it as a Microsoft product."

3. Camilla just stared. She had never heard of a computer bug that looked like an actual bug. She had certainly never heard a bug talk before. She didn't know what to say.

4. The bug sighed. "Cat got your tongue?" he asked.

5. "No-oo-ooo," said Camilla nervously. She looked around for a cat. If computer bugs could come out of the computer, then maybe cats really could grab a person's tongue.

6. "I'll make it easy for you," said the bug. "My name is Harold. You need to be nice to me. I can get inside your computer and make your life miserable. In fact, I can even give you this new Australian virus. It started near the Great Barrier Reef and quickly spread to computers in Sydney, then north to the United States and the rest of the world."

7. "Um..." said Camilla. She didn't want a computer virus, so she tried to be nice. She gave the bug a half-hearted smile. "Well... maybe I could buy Bug Attack, but I really just like playing Jupiter Space Race and Barbie the Fashion Astronaut."

8. The bug groaned. "Buy Bug Attack. It's only $583.00 and well worth the money. Your birthday is coming up on Saturday, November 11. You could ask for the game for a birthday present."

9. Camilla frowned. "My parents would never spend $583.00 on a birthday present! Even my rich Uncle Duke wouldn't spend that much on me."

10. "Too bad," said the Harold, gesturing toward the monitor. More bugs crawled out and started walking all over everything. "Here are some of my friends. Maybe they can talk you into this."

11. "I don't have the money!" cried Camilla.

12. "But you have a rich Uncle Duke," said the bug. "What does he do?"

13. "He is president of the United Conglomeration of Conglomerates. He works in the Empire State Building," she began.

14. "Tell me more." The bugs looked eager.

15. "Well...he's Catholic. He likes to go to the opera. *The Barber of Seville* is his favorite opera. He also likes old reruns of 'The Brady Bunch.' He's married. He has three children and a frog."

16. "Frogs! Yuk!" cried the bugs. "We hate frogs."

17. Camilla smiled a wicked grin. "Well, then you probably won't like Calvin, my frog. Just a minute and I'll get him."

18. The bugs hightailed it back into the monitor.

Write:

Answers will vary. Here are some possibilities.

Harold the computer bug was very frustrated. His Aunt Gladys told him he would never be good at anything, and he was beginning to think that was true. He thought to himself, "I can't even bully a little girl. What kind of computer bug am I?" His cousin Melissa was already a famous computer bug that had brought big corporations to their knees. He was in school with a bug named Love Bug Virus. He thought, "Some things never change. Love Bug Virus was the most popular computer bug in school, with the girls and everybody. Now, he's the most famous computer bug in the entire world."

As usual, Harold felt like a failure. He needed direction in his life, so he bought two books: *Other Careers for Computer Bugs* and *I Am Good Just Because I'm a Computer Bug*. Reading these books made Harold realize that he didn't need to cause mayhem in the world to make a name for himself.

He renamed himself the Gregory Hines Virus. Instead of destroying computers, he decided to entertain computer users. When someone downloaded him, he would tap dance on the screen. All it took was a couple of people to forward him to all of their friends, and Harold was an instant sensation. He made the front page of the *New York Times*, and they talked about him every hour on CNN's "Headline News." Harold, now known as the Gregory Hines Virus, had finally found his way.

Printed in the United States
by Baker & Taylor Publisher Services